bee

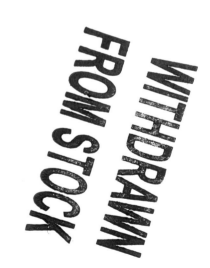

by

Ting Morris

illustrated by

Desiderio Sanzi

designed by

Deb Miner

W

FRANKLIN WATTS
LONDON • SYDNEY

You are in a patch of clover, where brightly-coloured flowers grow. Lots of bees are buzzing about.

Watch them land on the sweet-smelling clover. See them fly in and out of the flowers. Count them coming and going. What are they doing and where do they live?

Turn the page and take a closer look.

The bees' nest is in this hollow tree trunk.

It is the home of a colony of wild honeybees, and on this warm summer's day, there is a stream of workers flying in and out.

If you ever spot a bees' nest, don't go too close. Bees get very angry if their home is disturbed and will sting to defend themselves.

THE NEST

Wild honeybees usually make their nests in rock caves or hollow trees. Some nests may have up to 60,000 bees. Inside the nest, the bees build wax combs. The combs are upright sheets covered on both sides with thousands of tiny rooms called wax cells.

UNDERGROUND

Bumblebees are different from honeybees. They make their nests underground, sometimes in an old mouse nest. Between 20 and 150 bees live in a bumblebee nest.

WAX-WORKERS

Worker bees make wax in their glands, and it comes out through small holes in their bodies. They pick off the tiny white flakes of wax with their legs, chew them, and put the wax on the walls of the cells they are building.

SIX-SIDED CELLS

Each cell has six sides, and all the cells fit together perfectly. In some cells, the bees raise their young. In others, they store honey and pollen. The cell walls are tilted so that the honey can't run out.

A WORKER BEE'S BODY

A bee's body has three parts – the HEAD, the THORAX and the ABDOMEN, which includes a honey stomach. A bee carries nectar in its honey stomach. A bee's whole body is covered with furry hairs. The black and yellow stripes are warning colours.

A bee has five EYES: a big one on each side of its head, and three small ones on top.

Bees pick up smells with their FEELERS (called antennae).

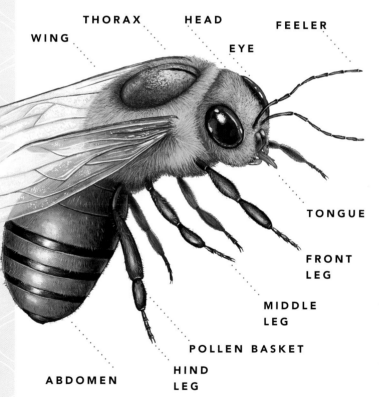

THORAX   HEAD   FEELER

WING   EYE

TONGUE

ABDOMEN   HIND LEG   POLLEN BASKET   MIDDLE LEG   FRONT LEG

The TONGUE is a long tube used to suck up water, nectar and honey. Bees hold wax and pollen with their jaws.

A bee has two pairs of WINGS, and it can fly forwards, backwards, sideways and hover in the air.

A bee uses the combs on its back LEGS to scrape pollen into POLLEN BASKETS on the outside of its back legs.

7

There's no relaxing in the sunshine for these workers. **They are the field bees in charge of finding and collecting food for the colony.** They fly out to flowers and bring back pollen and nectar.

The guards at the nest entrance know every bee in the nest and keep out unwelcome strangers. They kill enemies with their stings. Look at the bee loaded with yellow pollen. She has good news. There's a patch of sweet clover and foxgloves nearby!

WHO LIVES IN THE COLONY?

Honeybees are social insects. They live in large family groups and they all share the work.

THE QUEEN She is the biggest bee and does nothing but stay at home and lay eggs. The queen is the mother of all the bees in the nest.

BARBED STING!

A worker bee has a barbed, poisonous sting. If it digs into an enemy, the bee will die because the barbs hold tight and rip out its abdomen. But the queen can sting a number of times because she has a smooth, curved sting.

SMELLS RIGHT

All the bees in a nest have the same smell, because they all eat the same food. If a bee with the wrong smell tries to get in, the guards drive her away. There are many animals that like to steal their honey.

WORKERS They are smaller female bees who serve the queen. Field bees collect food for the colony and house bees work in the nest.

DRONES They are the male bees. Their only job is to fertilize the queen during her mating flight.

9

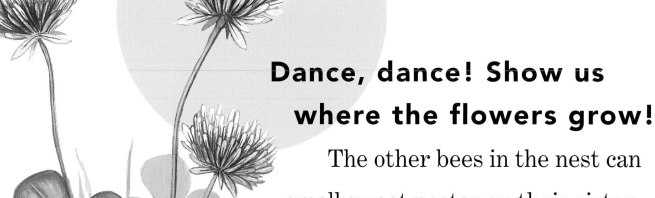

Dance, dance! Show us where the flowers grow!

The other bees in the nest can smell sweet nectar on their sister. She is dancing round and round on the comb to tell her nest-mates where she found clover and flowers. She goes faster and faster. Now the bees know that there's lots of food close to the nest. They join in the dance and learn the way to the clover patch.

MAKING A BEELINE

When a field worker finds flowers, she makes a beeline for the nest by flying straight there. Her smell tells the other bees which flowers to look for.

WAGGLE DANCE

If the food is far away, the bee waggles her abdomen and dances up and down inside the nest. She turns left and right to make a figure of eight and shows how far away the food is by the length of the straight runs and the number of waggles. The faster she waggles, the more nectar there is. Bees find the flowers by the sun. A straight run upwards means that the food is towards the sun. A straight run downwards means that it's away from the sun.

ROUND DANCE

If the food is near the nest, the field bee dances in circles. She moves around clockwise and anticlockwise on the combs. The faster she dances, the more flowers there are. The other bees follow her steps, and by copying her movements they learn the way to the flowers.

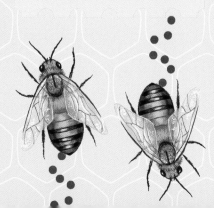

11

FLOWER POWER

Flowers attract insects with their sweet smell and bright colours. They do this because they need bees and other insects to carry pollen grains, which are made by a flower's male parts, to the eggs made by the female parts. Bees visit different flowers and mix the pollen and the eggs. This process is called pollination, and it helps plants to make seeds that grow into other plants.

Once they are sure of the way, hundreds of field bees zoom off to the clover patch. **The best time to get nectar is when the sun is high and the flowers are fully open.** The flight path is busy, with honeybees buzzing back and forth. A message from the nest calls for extra supplies of poppy pollen. That means there's no rest for the field workers!

12

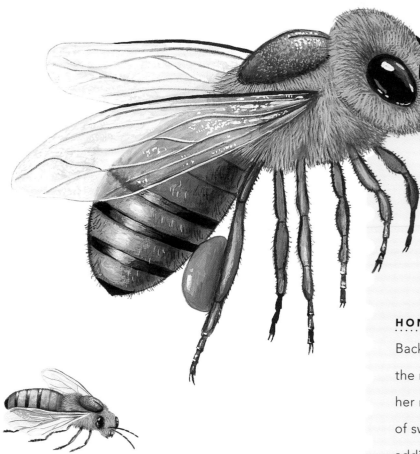

SWEET NECTAR

Nectar is a sweet, sugary liquid in flower blossoms. Bees suck it up, and during the flight home they store it inside their bodies in a pouch called a honey stomach.

HONEY, HONEY

Back in the nest, the field bee brings up the nectar, and a house bee sucks it from her mouth. The house bee chews the blob of sweet liquid for about 20 minutes, adding enzymes (chemicals that change the nectar). She stores the fluid in open cells and chews it again after a while. In the warm nest, the nectar dries out and turns into honey. Three days later, the house bee packs the honey into cells and seals them with a cap of wax. Honey is the bees' food supply.

HONEYCOMB

Combs with cells full of honey are called honeycombs. You can buy pieces of honeycomb – they taste delicious!

POLLEN BASKETS

Field bees collect pollen and nectar. Pollen is the fine, powdery dust in flowers. It gets caught on the bee's hairy body when she walks over the flowers to suck the nectar. She combs the grains into the pollen baskets on her back legs. Pollen is an important food for young, growing bees.

Inside the nest, the queen bee is served by her female workers.

She has just let them know that she'd like some poppy pollen for herself and the grubs. This information is passed on from nurse bees to house bees and finally to the field bees.

The bees have to work hard because the queen is laying more than 1,000 eggs a day. Cells have to be cleaned, new cells have to be built, and more honey has to be made.

BUSY TONGUES

Messages are passed around the whole colony because bees share food all the time. They pass nectar to each other through their tongues.

ROYAL MESSAGE

The queen bee makes special chemicals in glands around her mouth to pass information on to other bees. Her female workers lick these liquid messages when they feed the queen.

DIFFERENT JOBS

In the summer, a worker bee lives for only about six weeks. During that time she takes on different duties.

WEEK 1

First she is a cleaner, preparing cells for new eggs. After three days, she becomes a nurse, feeding pollen and honey to the grubs.

WEEK 2

On the sixth day, she starts to feed the queen and the larvae with royal jelly. She does this job for about a week. Then she becomes a builder of wax cells.

WEEKS 3-6

Around the 16th day, she starts to work in the storerooms. She takes in nectar and pollen from the field bees, and turns the nectar into honey. On about the 20th day, she stands guard at the nest entrance. From the third week until the end of her life, she is a field bee collecting food.

15

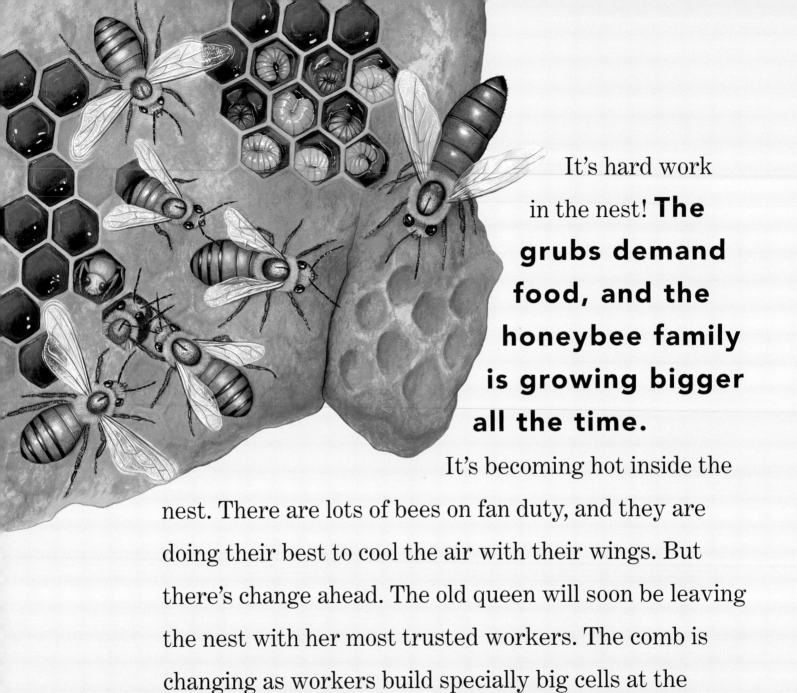

It's hard work in the nest! **The grubs demand food, and the honeybee family is growing bigger all the time.**

It's becoming hot inside the nest. There are lots of bees on fan duty, and they are doing their best to cool the air with their wings. But there's change ahead. The old queen will soon be leaving the nest with her most trusted workers. The comb is changing as workers build specially big cells at the edge. New queens will grow inside these cells.

QUEEN CELLS

Queen cells are bigger than worker cells. Royal grubs are fed only royal jelly. After 16 days, a big baby queen emerges.

ROYAL JELLY

This creamy food is full of vitamins. It comes from glands in the heads of nurse bees. The queen bee and queen grubs live on it.

FROM EGG TO BEE

When a queen has mated with a male bee (called a drone), she can lay eggs for the rest of her life. The queen has ruled this nest for three years.

The queen lays one egg inside each cell.

After three days, the egg hatches into a larva, or grub. For the first three days, all the grubs are fed royal jelly by nurse bees.

Nurse bees feed the grubs bee bread, mixed honey and pollen.

After five days, the nurses seal the cells with wax lids.

Inside its wax cell, each grub becomes a pupa and spins a covering of silk called a cocoon.

Gradually the grub takes on colour.

A baby worker bee chews its way out of its wax cell 21 days after the egg was laid.

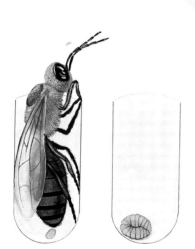
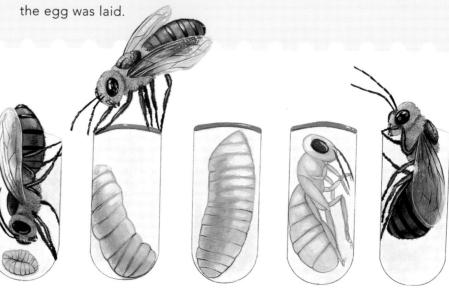

17

NEST-HUNTING

Scout bees dance to tell other scouts to look at possible nesting places. They check out each other's finds. After much buzzing about, they decide on a place and move in to start a new colony.

A queen knows when it's time to leave the old nest. Soon there will be no room for her in this crowded colony. She knows that her workers are feeding young queens, and her trusted servants are ready for the journey. They have filled themselves with honey and are waiting for her outside the nest.

Together they fly off to a nearby tree.

The swarm settles on a branch while scouts search for a new nesting site. When a scout finds a good place, she dances to show the others where it is.

SWARMING

The bees' flight to start a new colony is called swarming. This usually happens when the nest becomes too full or when the queen is too old to lay enough eggs. The workers then build big cells for new queens to grow in. Just before the young queens are ready, the old queen gives the signal to leave. About half the workers gather outside the nest and wait for their queen to come out. They cluster around her and fly up into the air.

19

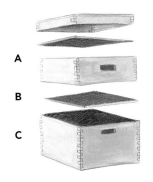

A MODERN BEEHIVE

Modern hives are wooden boxes with several drawer-like frames, called supers, that can be taken out. The bees build their combs in these. The lower section (**C**) is for the queen. The upper section (**A**) is for storing honey. The worker bees can reach all parts of the hive, but the queen is too big to fit through the grille (**B**) into the honeycomb. She can lay her eggs only in the cells at the bottom.

What an amazing find! A wooden box with a sturdy roof, and inside is a place waiting to be filled with honeycombs. The queen starts laying eggs at once. Soon the house bees are busy building and cleaning, while field bees bring pollen and nectar from sunflowers nearby. The bees don't know that the hive was built by a bee-keeper who will take away their honeycombs. But they are happy workers and make as much honey as they can.

HANDLE WITH CARE

When the bee-keeper takes out honeycombs, she must be careful to avoid being stung. She wears a wire screen to protect her face, and special clothes and gloves.

LONG AGO

People have been taking honey from bees for thousands of years. The first bee-keepers put straw baskets, called skeps, near their homes. Bees flew inside and built their combs on sticks.

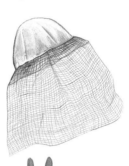

HONEYBEE SETTLERS

About 400 years ago, people from England took honeybees with them to America. Today bee-keepers look after millions of hives. Every year they produce about 91 million kilograms of honey. For every kilo of honey, bees collect nectar from more than two million flowers.

The old queen has gone. For a week, the new, young queen has been eating lots of honey to make her strong. She has killed her rivals in their cells, and now the nest is hers.

Today she is going on her mating flight. Look how she flies up into the sky. Lots of drones chase her. The young queen will choose the one that can fly the highest.

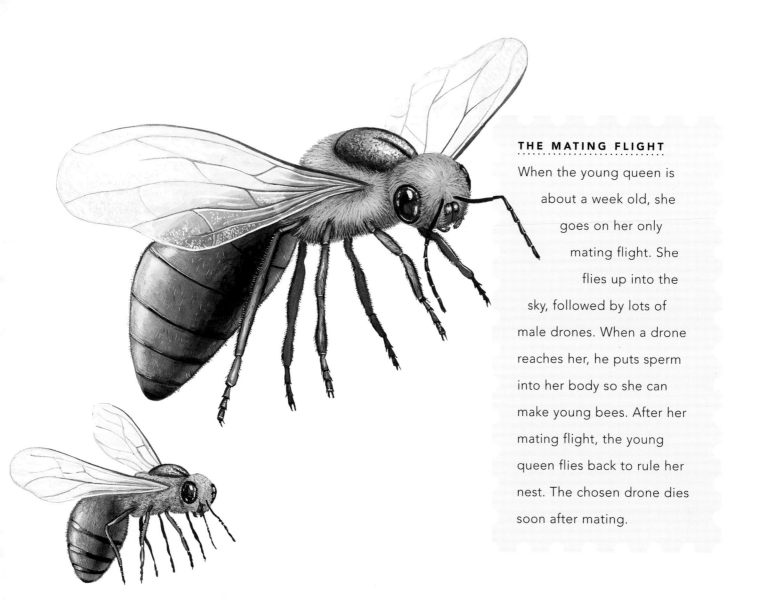

THE MATING FLIGHT

When the young queen is about a week old, she goes on her only mating flight. She flies up into the sky, followed by lots of male drones. When a drone reaches her, he puts sperm into her body so she can make young bees. After her mating flight, the young queen flies back to rule her nest. The chosen drone dies soon after mating.

UNLUCKY DRONES

The drones that don't mate with the queen go back to the nest and are fed by their sisters until the autumn. Then they are thrown out and die. Male bees can't feed themselves because their tongues are too short to reach nectar.

23

SPRING EGGS

In spring, the honeybee queen starts laying eggs again. The workers clean out old cells and build new ones for the growing grubs.

24

In wintertime, it's too cold for the honeybees to leave their nest. All the flowers have died, but the bees have stored enough honey to eat through the winter. Inside the nest, they huddle together and shake their wings to stay warm.

Perhaps the bees are dreaming o sunny days, beautiful flowers, sweet nectar and yellow pollen. When the first flowers open in spring, these honeybees will be buzzing about again.

BUMBLE QUEENS

Among bumblebees, only the queen lives through the winter. The rest of the colony dies. When the queen wakes up in the spring, she makes two pots using wax from her body. She fills one pot with honey and the other with eggs. She sits on the egg pot to keep it warm.

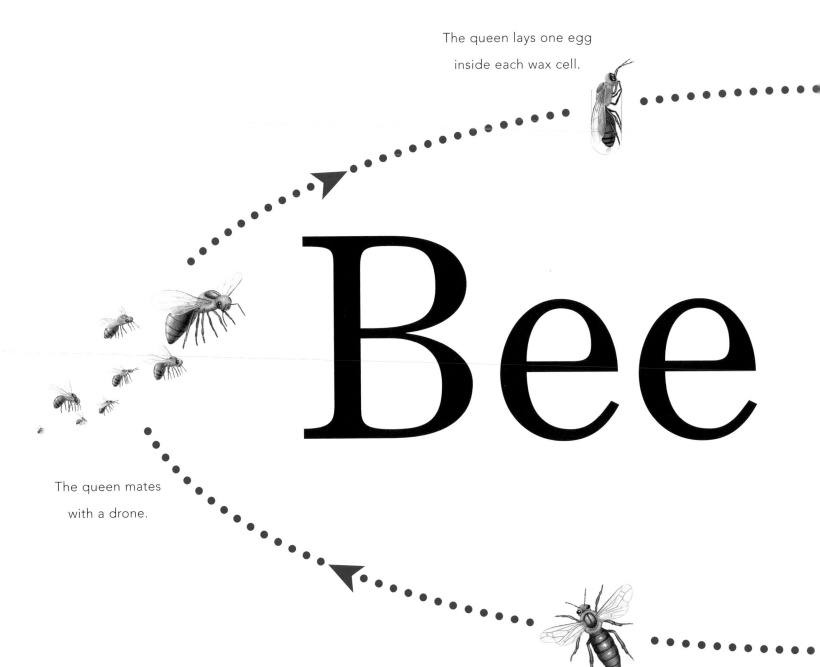

The queen lays one egg
inside each wax cell.

Bee

The queen mates
with a drone.

Honeybees share
work in the colony.

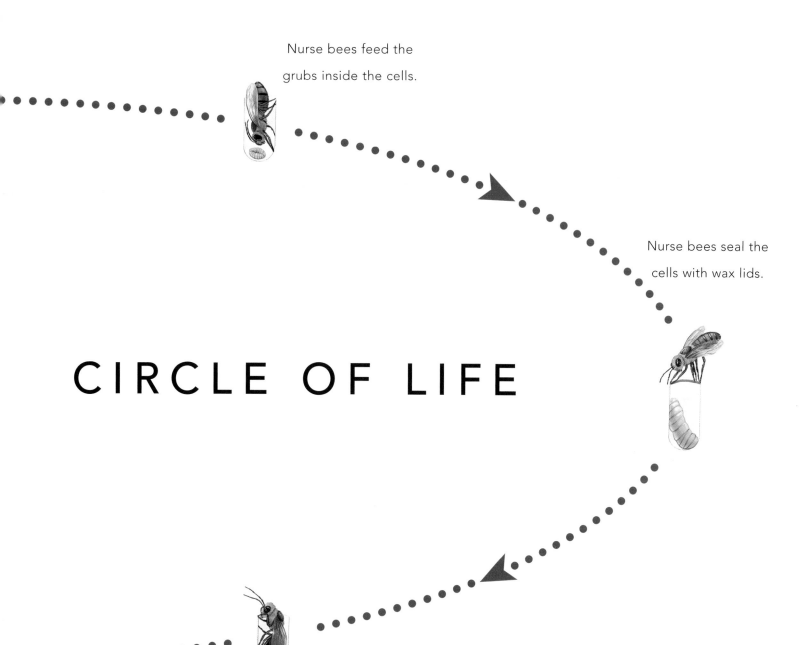

Nurse bees feed the
grubs inside the cells.

Nurse bees seal the
cells with wax lids.

CIRCLE OF LIFE

The young bees emerge
from their cocoons.

barb A barb is the pointed, angled part of a bee's sting that acts like a hook.

cocoon A silky case spun by insect larvae, which protects them while they grow into pupae.

glands Organs in an animal's body that produce important substances.

grubs The young form of some insects; another word for larvae.

hive An artificial nesting box for bees, from which bee-keepers collect honey.

hover To stay in one place in the air.

mating flight A flight made by queen bees when they mate with male bees.

nectar A sweet, sugary liquid produced by flowers.

nurse bees Bees that look after and feed young bees.

pollen Powdery, dust-like grains made by flowers.

pollination The process in which a plant's pollen is mixed with eggs to make seeds and new plants.

queen A large female bee that lays eggs; there is one queen in every nest.

royal jelly A substance produced by worker bees that is used to feed the larvae that will become future queen bees.

sperm Fluid produced by male animals that makes a female's eggs grow into young.

vitamins Substances found in food that animals need to stay healthy.

 An Appleseed Editions book

First published in 2004 by Franklin Watts
96 Leonard Street, London, EC2A 4XD

Franklin Watts Australia
45–51 Huntley Street, Alexandria, NSW 2015

© 2004 Appleseed Editions

Created by Appleseed Editions Ltd,
Well House, Friars Hill, Guestling, East Sussex, TN35 4ET

Illustrator: Desiderio Sanzi

Designer: Deb Miner

ISBN 0 7496 5705 7

A CIP catalogue for this book is available from the British Library.

Printed and bound in the USA

Head of Blind-worm. $^1/_2$

A Book-scorpion (*Chelifer cancroides*). $^5/_1$

Cotton-stainer

Proxys punctulatus.

Click-beetle, natural size.

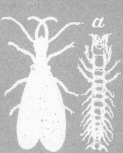

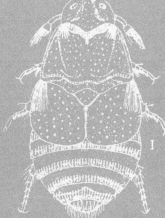

Epeiridæ.

a, male, and *b*, female, of *Epeira stellata*; *c*, characteristic orb-web of an epeirid (*Epeira strix*).

Parasite of the Beaver (*Platypsyllus castoris*). (Line shows natural size.)

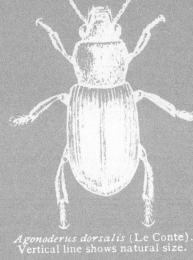

Agonoderus dorsalis (Le Conte). Vertical line shows natural size.

Hellgrammite (*a*) and Hellgrammite-fly.

The Twig-girdler (*Oncideres cingulata*). $^1/_1$

a, a branch girdled by the beetle.

Hawthorn-tingis (*arcuata*), one of the enlarged about ten

The Drag (*Dr* eatu

Sinea diadema, one of the *Reduviidæ*. (Line shows natural size.)

The Bait-bug.

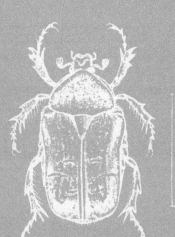

Rose-beetle (*Cetonia aurata*). Vertical line shows natural size.

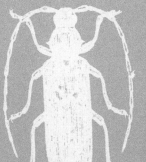

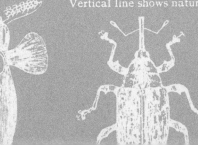

Flour-beetle (*T* *litor*). (Line sh size.)

A Species of *Phrynus*, about life-size.

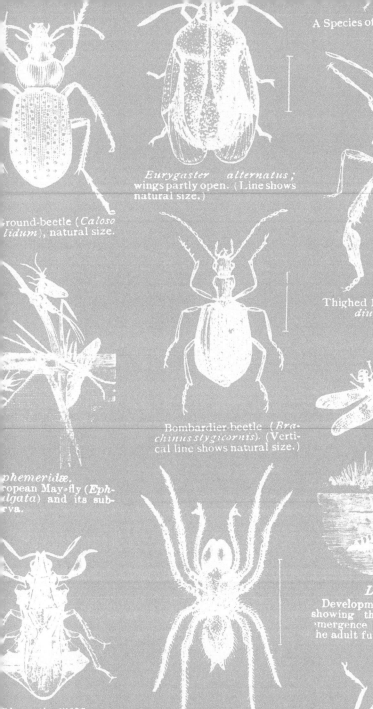

Eurygaster alternatus; wings partly open. (Line shows natural size.)

round-beetle (*Caloso lidum*), natural size.

Thighed Metapodius (*Metapodius femoratus*).

Spiderwort Owlet-moth (*Prodenia flavimedia*). *a*, larva; *b*, wings of moth.

Apple-
pul...
8, siphon...

The stem...
a, la...
ting...
ver...
the b...

The Cucujo.

Hor...
Tail of...
ing hom...
dal vert...
dal rays...
bones;...
esses of...
united to...
for the a...
ral spine

Bombardier-beetle (*Brachinus stygicornis*). (Vertical line shows natural size.)

phemeridæ.
ropean May-fly (*Eph-
lgata*) and its sub-
rva.

Libellulidæ.
Development of a dragon-fly, showing the subaquatic larva, emergence from the pupa, and the adult fully winged insect.

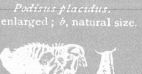

Podisus placidus.
a, enlarged; *b*, natural size.

A Flea (*Pulex irritans*).
a, puncturing stylets of the proboscis.

A Bristletail (*Lepisma saccharina*). 5/1

Phymata erosa.

Atypus sulzeri. (Vertical line shows natural size.)

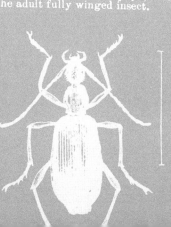

Grape-vine Fidia (*F. viticida*). (Line sh ws natural size.)

Bacon-
beet'e.

One of t

A De

Published by
Grandreams Limited
435-437 Edgware Road, Little Venice
London W2 1TH

Printed in Malaysia

50 BEDTIME STORIES

Written by Anne McKie
Illustrated by Ken McKie

CONTENTS

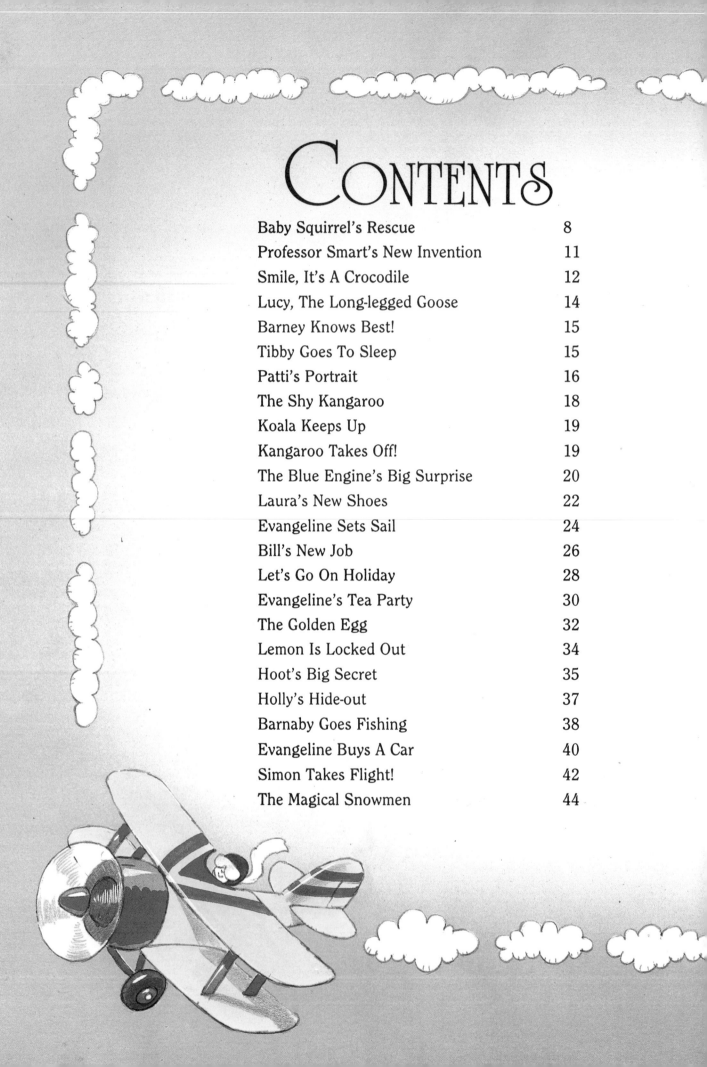

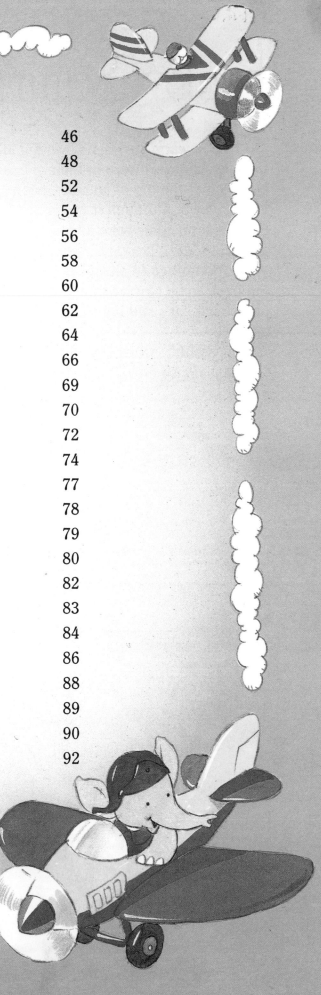

Baby Squirrel's Rescue

One warm summer's evening all the little squirrels were in their bedroom at the top of an oak tree in Forest Town. Although it was past their bedtime, they were all still wide awake.

"I can't go to sleep!" cried Baby Squirrel, as he bounced up and down on his bed. "It's still light and I want to play!"

"Ssshh!!" whispered the others. "Don't make so much noise or Mother will hear you, then we'll all be in trouble!"

"See if I care," Baby Squirrel giggled and bounced up and down even more.

When the other squirrels saw their young brother having so much fun, they decided to join in too. Very soon they were all jumping up and down on the bed and making a dreadful noise.

"Look at me," cried Baby Squirrel, "I can jump higher than any of you!"

All of a sudden, he bounced up into the air, through the open window and landed right on the top branch of the tallest tree in Forest Town. All the little squirrels rushed over to the window.

"Help! Help!" yelled Baby Squirrel as he swung to and fro. "Somebody get me down!"

Just at that very moment, Mother Squirrel burst in through the bedroom door. She had heard all the noise and came to find out what was going on. When she looked out of the window and saw her baby hanging onto the topmost branch of the tallest tree in Forest Town, she could hardly believe her eyes.

"How did you get up there?" she cried in surprise. "Come back in here this minute!" Poor Baby Squirrel was too frightened to reply.

"I can't reach up there!" Mother Squirrel called as she looked up into the branches. "I must send for the Forest Town Fire Brigade."

When the firemen arrived, they looked up into the tall tree and shook

their heads. "Our ladders aren't long enough to reach him," said the Forest Town Fire Chief. "He'll have to jump!"

"Jump?!" screamed Mother Squirrel with fright. All the little squirrels began to cry.

"Don't worry one bit," smiled the Fire Chief as the team of firemen held open a very big safety sheet.

Now when Baby Squirrel looked down into the safety sheet far below, he wasn't a bit afraid. "I'll pretend I'm bouncing on my bed," he called to the firemen. "Watch out, here I come!"

Baby Squirrel flew through the air and landed in the safety sheet quite unharmed.

"That was marvellous!" squealed Baby Squirrel with delight. "Can I do it again?"

"Certainly not!" snapped his mother. "Off to bed with you and no more bouncing up and down."

That night the little squirrels dreamt they were firemen. Baby Squirrel, meanwhile, was dreaming of flying through the air on a trapeze at the circus!

Professor Smart's New Invention

Jack lived next door to Professor Smart. One night, when the Professor's lights were on very late, Jack guessed he would be inventing something.

"Come and look at my new car!" the Professor shouted to Jack over the garden fence the next morning.

But Jack didn't have to go anywhere because the car came to him! It drove up one side of the fence, across the top and down the other side.

"It's a remote controlled car," Jack gasped, "what a beauty!"

The little blue car shot across the flowerbeds, straight through the greenhouse and out the other side. Then it climbed up the garden step and through the stone fountain.

"I'd better catch it before it wrecks Dad's prize dahlias!" cried Jack.

The little remote controlled car certainly had caused havoc.

"Help Jack!" cried the Professor. "Catch it if you can!"

As he ran past the garden shed, Jack had a bright idea. He grabbed his dad's large fishing net and scooped up the car in a moment.

"Thank goodness!" the Professor sighed with relief. "The car works perfectly, but I haven't invented a way to stop it yet!"

"I think you'd better do that right away," laughed Jack, as he handed back the car, "before it does any more damage!"

Smile, It's A Crocodile

There once was a very friendly crocodile. He loved meeting people, talking and going out to parties.

Sad to say, he didn't meet many people, so he hardly ever talked to anyone, and he never got asked to parties! Now why do you think that was?

The crocodile was so nice and friendly that he smiled all the time. And when he smiled, he showed his teeth - rows and rows of sharp pointed teeth that sparkled in the sun.

If you smiled at a crocodile and he smiled back, would you go up and shake his hand just to be friendly?

Oh no, you'd run away as fast as you could! And this, unfortunately, was just what happened. Every single time the crocodile smiled, people would run away, they never smiled back.

One day, the poor crocodile was so lonely, he took a walk into town. He smiled nicely at everyone he met. He even grinned at every single person in a bus queue, but not one of them

smiled back. Instead, they fled in all directions.

"Oh dear!" exclaimed the crocodile. "They've missed their bus!"

Then all alone, he walked into a store and smiled politely at the assistants. Most of them dived behind the counter and one of them climbed on top of the shelves!

"Oh dear!" said the crocodile, looking around. "Where have all the customers gone?"

Feeling rather glum, he walked a little further down the street. He hadn't gone very far before a man in a white coat came running towards him.

"I'll try to be nice just once more," said the crocodile, grinning widely and showing every one of his sharp pointed teeth.

The man didn't just smile back, he threw his arms around the crocodile and did a little dance in the middle of the street.

"What a beautiful smile!" cried the man in delight. "I am a dentist and you must have the best set of teeth I have ever seen!"

The crocodile went quite red.

"Please come and be my new model and assistant!" begged the dentist. "You can show everyone how to brush their teeth properly, then they'll have a sparkling smile just like yours!"

Of course, the crocodile said yes. Soon, people came flooding to the dentist, just to see a crocodile brushing his teeth.

Now, everyone smiles at the crocodile and he smiles back proudly, his rows and rows of teeth sparkling even more with all that brushing!

Lucy, The Long-legged Goose

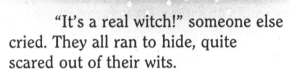

It was Halloween and everyone in the farmyard was getting very excited. The animals were looking forward to a very special party that night, but most of all they were looking forward to dressing up.

"I'm going as a Red Indian!" grunted the pig.

"Then I'll be a cowboy!" giggled the goat.

"And what will you be?" the farmer asked Lucy, the long-legged goose.

"It's a secret!" honked Lucy as she scurried across the farmyard. Now Lucy the goose had been planning her costume for weeks and wanted it to be a great surprise.

Late that night, when the moon was full and everyone was at the party, a dark shadow flitted across the sky.

"A witch!" someone gasped. Everyone looked up. There, high above the trees, was a witch on a broomstick circling round ready to swoop down on the animals in the farmyard.

"It's a real witch!" someone else cried. They all ran to hide, quite scared out of their wits.

The witch's broomstick landed in the middle of the farmyard with a thump. One by one the animals peered from their hiding places and then began to laugh.

"It's not a witch at all!" they roared.

"It's Lucy the long-legged goose! I'd know those bright yellow legs anywhere!" chuckled the farmer.

Barney Knows Best!

Lisa had a brand new winter outfit. "What great clothes," said Lisa proudly. "I shall never take them off!"

Her little dog, Barney, sniggered because he knew that she would have to soon enough!

"I shall wear my new outfit in the rain, in the snow and when the cold wind blows. I shall never ever take it off!"

Her little dog, Barney, smiled to himself and gazed up into the sky.

The sun came out from behind a cloud and soon it felt very warm.

"Phew!" gasped Lisa. "I'll have to take off this outfit and find a cooler one!"

Her little dog, Barney, chuckled to himself, "I just knew she would!"

Tibby Goes To Sleep

Philip's cat, Tibby, sleeps anywhere - in a cardboard box or the back of a chair! She sleeps in the strangest of places all over the house, and no-one can find her when it's time to go out.

When the family get up in the morning, if nobody is looking, she will creep into someone's warm bed and stay there all morning!

Philip is getting ready for his first day at a new school. He would like to say goodbye to Tibby, but as usual, she is nowhere to be found.

Perhaps Philip won't miss Tibby at school as much as he thinks!

Patti's Portrait

Patti the pig was wandering through the meadow one fine, summer morning. She paused for a minute to smell the flowers and gaze up into the clear, blue sky.

"What a lovely morning," she sighed, "and what beautiful, beautiful flowers."

"And what a beautiful pig!" said a voice from behind.

Patti turned round, rather startled. There, sitting in the long grass, was an artist painting a picture.

"I've never seen a more beautiful pig," the artist went on, "I simply must paint your picture!"

"How wonderful," squealed Patti, very thrilled. "But I've absolutely nothing to wear!" And before the artist could stop her, she trotted away at top speed.

Very soon, Patti the pig returned to the farm and quietly tiptoed into the farmhouse. No-one was in, so she crept upstairs. She searched inside cupboards and drawers until she found a hat and a dress, a necklace and some shoes that belonged to the farmer's wife.

"Perfect!" Patti sighed as she gazed in the mirror. "I really am the most beautiful pig!"

When the artist saw Patti, he shook his head. "Where is that beautiful pig that I met in the meadow this morning?"

"I'm here!" squealed Patti. "I've dressed up for the picture!"

"No need," replied the artist, "you were quite exquisite before!"

So, Patti carefully folded up the farmer's wife's clothes, then stood very still in the meadow sniffing the flowers.

When the artist had finished his painting, he hung it in an art gallery. One day he took Patti along to see for herself what a very beautiful picture she made!

The Shy Kangaroo

"It's hard to make friends when you're shy. But it's worth it, so give it a try..." the shy little kangaroo's mother told him every day. But the little kangaroo was far too shy to jump out of his mother's pouch, instead he just peeped over the top.

One day he almost made it, but a noisy cockatoo screeched, "How are you?" so loudly in his ear, that he jumped back in his mother's pouch and would not come out again.

"You're missing all the fun," whispered his mother. "Come out and find a friend!"

Now a koala who lived in the trees above could see the little kangaroo hiding inside his mother's pouch, and he really did want to be his friend.

He thought for a long time and at last came up with an idea he thought might work. He came down from the trees, stood in front of Mother Kangaroo and stared at the ground.

The koala stayed in exactly the same spot all morning, just staring down.

The shy little kangaroo watched him for hours, his head just peeping out of his mother's pouch. At last, he simply had to find out what the koala was staring at.

All at once he jumped out of the pouch and landed right in front of the koala.

"Will you be my friend?" asked the koala as he hugged the little kangaroo.

"If you will tell me what you are looking at on the ground," whispered the little kangaroo.

"Nothing at all!" giggled the koala, "but it made you come out of your mother's pouch to find out. Now you're not shy any more!"

Koala Keeps Up

Kangaroo and Koala were the very best of friends and spent lots of time together. They liked to go to the country, they liked to visit the town, and anywhere else that took their fancy...but there was just one problem!

Kangaroo could travel very quickly hopping along at speed, but poor Koala couldn't keep up.

"Don't leave me behind!" he puffed. "I can't run very fast, my legs are too short!"

Kangaroo thought for a while. "I know just the thing!" he laughed. "Now you'll never get left behind!"

Kangaroo Takes Off!

"How high can you jump?" Koala asked his friend Kangaroo, as he looked down from the top of his tree.

"Higher than the fence and nearly as high as the branch of your tree," he replied.

"But you can't reach me," cried Koala.

"I know and it would be very useful if I had something important to tell you," said Kangaroo.

Koala gave the problem some thought. "I know now you can reach me when I'm in my tree any time you want!" he laughed.

The Blue Engine's Big Surprise

One day a visitor came to look around the huge sheds at the railway station where the trains were kept.

"I am looking for a special engine," he told the stationmaster. "I need an engine that is not too big and not too small. I need an engine that is strong enough to pull lots of wagons a long way!"

"The Little Blue Engine over there is just what you want," said the stationmaster, "but I'm afraid he is a little rusty and some of his wagons are falling to pieces!"

"Don't worry one bit!" the visitor told the stationmaster. "I shall take care of everything!"

The Little Blue Engine was very pleased. He had been standing in the railway station shed for a long time with no-one to talk to and nothing to do.

The very next morning, a gang of people arrived. They scrubbed and rubbed and polished the Little Blue Engine's paintwork and cleaned all the brass until it sparkled and shone. Then they set to work mending and

painting all the wagons and carriages. The Little Blue Engine had never looked so smart.

'I wonder when the passengers will arrive and where I will be taking them,' thought the Engine. It was all very exciting!

He didn't have to wait long to find out. Very soon the driver climbed aboard and the Little Blue Engine pulled out of the shed and whistled goodbye to the other trains left behind.

As he pulled into the station, he heard the announcer saying, "The train arriving at platform one is the new circus train to take the Big Top Circus anywhere it wants to go. Goodbye Little Blue Engine and good luck!"

Laura's New Shoes

Laura loved new shoes. She loved going to the shoe shop and taking ages to choose her favourite pair. Then she loved walking home in her new shoes, carrying her old ones back in a cardboard box.

One day her mother said, "Laura, the toes of your shoes are scuffed and the heels look a little worn. Put on your coat and we'll go to the shop to choose some new ones!"

The shoe shop was empty, so Laura could take her time to look around at all the new styles and different colours.

At last her mother said, "Laura, you have had lots of time to choose, which pair would you like?"

Laura sighed. She loved the shiny patent leather ones with the ankle straps and silver buckles. She thought the pink shoes decorated with tiny hearts and fastened with pearl buttons were simply wonderful. But most of all she really wanted the red and yellow shoes with fancy laces.

"Laura," said her mother. "Have you made up your mind?"

Laura took a deep breath and pointed to some dull brown slip-on shoes hidden at the bottom of the racks.

"I'll have that pair," whispered Laura, "and I would like to leave my old shoes on and carry the new ones home in the box!"

Inside the box was a doll. Not an ordinary doll, but a doll with laces and buttons and bows, even zips, all over her clothes.

"If you practise on this special doll, you'll soon learn to fasten anything!"

And that is exactly what Laura did. So, the next time she went shopping to buy shoes, Laura chose just what she really wanted!

The rest of that day, Laura was very quiet. She took her new shoes upstairs and put them in her wardrobe. She didn't even try them on, but kept them shut away in the cardboard box.

"Laura," said her mother as she put her to bed that night, "why did you choose such a dull pair of shoes?"

Poor Laura looked miserable. "All the nicest shoes in the shop had buckles, bows or buttons, and I can't fasten any of those!"

How Laura's mother laughed. "Is that all?" she said. "I know an easy way to learn, but you will have to wait until tomorrow to find out!"

Early next morning, Laura's mother went to the shops, but she didn't take Laura. When she returned she was carrying a parcel in fancy wrapping paper.

"Is it a present for me?" asked Laura eagerly.

"Open it and see," replied her mother.

Evangeline Sets Sail

One day Evangeline the china doll and her friends went to the pond for a picnic. As they sat on the grass eating their lunch, they watched the boats sailing across the boating lake.

"I would like to go for a sail," said Evangeline as she reached for the last chocolate biscuit.

The sailor doll and the others had a wonderful time skimming across the water all afternoon. As for Evangeline, she stayed in the same spot for hours.

"Do you need any help?" the sailor doll shouted as he sped by.

"That's a good idea!" said the sailor doll jumping up quickly. "We'll hire a boat right away!"

"I want that one with the big striped sail!" shouted Evangeline as the sailor doll crossed the grass. "You others can share the small boat!"

"Have you ever sailed before, Evangeline?" asked the blue rabbit.

"Lots of times!" snapped Evangeline as she floated away in the biggest boat.

"None at all!" Evangeline yelled back tossing her head in the air.

All of a sudden, she overbalanced and fell overboard and her boat floated away to the other side of the lake.

"Help! Help!" Evangeline screamed as she thrashed about in the water. "It's very cold and my curls are getting wet! Get me out at once!"

"I thought you were a good sailor!" laughed the sailor doll as he steered his boat towards her. The others were giggling too!

"Stop laughing at once!" screamed Evangeline. "If you don't rescue me, I shall drown!"

This made her friends laugh so much that they almost upset their boat. That part of the lake was very shallow and everyone knew that if Evangeline stood up, she would be quite safe.

"You're in no danger at all!" smiled the sailor doll. And when Evangeline stopped splashing about and stood up, the water came just above her knees. The sailor doll helped Evangeline into the boat with all the others.

"Why did you make such a fuss?" asked the blue rabbit.

"How was I to know that the water wasn't deep?" cried Evangeline dripping wet. "You see, I can't swim!"

Everyone gasped. "You can't swim?" they all chorused. "Then you must learn straight away!"

Now, how Evangeline learnt to swim is another story...

Bill's New Job

Once upon a time there was a very nice man named Bill. He worked in an office, but found his job very tiresome.

"Oh dear!" sighed Bill, at the end of a very long dull week, "I really must look for another job, one a bit more exciting!"

So, that very day, he put away his pens, said goodbye to everybody in the office and left.

"What job shall I do now?" Bill asked himself, as he walked home. "Shall I be a farmer, or a baker, or a bus driver, or a bricklayer?" Bill wondered if he needed special training for these jobs. Suddenly, he thought of a marvellous idea, "I'll be a burglar! - that's sure to be different!"

So that day, Bill went to the library and took out a book called *How To Be A Successful Burglar.*

'You will need soft shoes to walk on tiptoe, a mask to disguise your face, a powerful torch to use on pitch-black nights, a rope ladder to climb in and out of tall buildings...' the book said, '...and a big sack to carry the loot.'

"Oh dear me," gasped Bill. "I hate heights and I'm afraid of the dark, but I do want to be a burglar." He thought for a while, "I know I'll go out in the daytime!"

The very next morning, Bill took some money out of his bank account and bought all the things he needed to be a real burglar.

The afternoon was bright and sunny. "What a lovely day for my very first burglary," said Bill, so straight away he set off down the road with his mask on his face and a huge sack slung over his shoulder.

As Bill walked through the town, people came out of the banks and shops to say hello to their friend as he passed by. "How can I be a burglar with this crowd behind me?" said Bill, rather surprised.

At last, they reached the town hall and the Mayor himself came out to greet Bill. "What a wonderful costume!" laughed the Mayor as he handed Bill an enormous silver cup. "You have just won first prize in this afternoon's fancy dress competition! Well done!"

Everybody cheered, but Bill looked a bit glum. "I'll never make a burglar!" he sighed. "Everyone has recognised me and now I don't have a job!"

Poor Bill took off his burglar's mask and sat down on the steps of the town hall.

"Would you like a job working for me?" asked the Mayor, who saw how downhearted Bill looked. "I need someone to drive my long black car and look after my golden regalia!"

Bill agreed at once. He put on his brand new chauffeur's uniform and while no-one was looking, threw the burglar's outfit into the nearest dustbin!

Let's Go On Holiday

Very early one morning, the zoo keeper put a notice on the gates of the zoo which read, *Closed For Two Weeks' Holiday*.

The animals were most surprised and wondered what to do.

"We need a holiday," said the keeper, "but don't worry, someone will come to look after you."

The animals looked around in dismay. "But we need a holiday too," they muttered amongst themselves.

There and then, some of the animals agreed to pack their bags, walk through the zoo gates and go to the seaside.

They hadn't gone very far before some of the little ones began to feel tired. "Are we near yet?" asked the smallest monkey, "it's a long way to the seaside and my feet hurt already."

So everyone sat down for a rest. Just then, around the corner came Ellie Elephant. "Jump on my back and I will take you all to the seaside. I'll be your taxi and we'll be there in next to no time!"

28

"Three cheers for Ellie!" the animals cried, "and three cheers for our holiday!"

Evangeline's Tea Party

One day Evangeline the china doll thought she would give a tea party. So right away, she made lots of tiny iced buns and plenty of dainty sandwiches. She made a jug of lemonade and one of orange, then put them in the refrigerator to cool.

Next she set out all the garden furniture and last of all put up her huge yellow sun umbrella, just to keep the hot sun from spoiling the tiny cakes and wafer thin sandwiches.

"Oh dear!" sighed all her neighbours. "Evangeline is giving one of her tea parties. They're so very dull. Everybody has to be on their best behaviour and sit still all afternoon!"

"Hurry up everyone!" called Evangeline, in her loudest voice. "Sit up straight and don't put your elbows on the table!" Evangeline could be very bossy at times.

All of a sudden, a strong gust of wind blew the yellow sun umbrella up into the air. It went flying over the roof-tops, through the park and into the field beyond.

Poor Evangeline jumped up and down in temper. "My tea party is ruined!" she screamed. "Go after my umbrella at once."

So all her friends ran across the field to try and catch up with Evangeline's yellow sun umbrella.

"Isn't this fun?" gasped the sailor doll, quite out of breath. "Evangeline's tea party isn't dull after all!"

At last they caught up with the yellow sun umbrella - and where do you think it was? Upside down in Farmer Jones' duck pond!

"Get it out at once!" screamed Evangeline, having one of her tantrums. "It will get all wet and muddy!"

"There, there, young lady," said Farmer Jones, trying not to laugh. "My ducks will get it out for you."

"My tea party is ruined!" sobbed poor Evangeline. "My cakes will have melted in the hot sun and the sandwiches will be all curly at the edges!"

By the time the ducks had floated the yellow sun umbrella to the edge of the pond, everyone was feeling very hungry.

"Come and have tea with us," suggested the farmer's wife with a wink, "but I'm afraid it won't be dainty cakes and tiny sandwiches!"

Soon everyone was tucking in to a huge spread of bread and cheese, pies and pastries. They all enjoyed a wonderful farmhouse tea, especially Evangeline, who surprised everyone by eating far more than anyone else!

The Golden Egg

There was once a little brown hen who laid eggs on a nest of straw in a corner of the farmyard. They were big brown eggs and the farmer's wife always collected them very carefully in her basket.

Now the little brown hen was not at all content with sitting on her nest of straw laying brown eggs.

"I wish I could lay golden eggs!" she sighed, "or just one would do, then I would be happy!"

Some of the other hens scratching in the farmyard overheard what the little brown hen had said and they began to cluck. "She wants to lay golden eggs!" they said. "Brown eggs aren't good enough for her!"

The hens made so much noise that all the animals in the farmyard heard. This made the poor little brown hen feel rather silly as she sat on her nest laying eggs for breakfast.

Now when the farmer's wife found out about the little brown hen's wish, she smiled to herself, for she knew exactly what to do.

As it was springtime and very near to Easter, everyone was looking forward to brightly coloured eggs. So, the farmer's wife took a basket of big brown eggs and painted and decorated them in wonderful patterns, except for the biggest brown egg, which she sprayed with shiny gold paint.

Later, when she went to collect the eggs, she slipped the golden egg underneath the little brown hen.

After a while, when the little brown hen hopped off her nest, she turned and saw the glittering golden egg.

She made such a noise that everyone in the farmyard came rushing over. "My wish has been granted," she clucked. "I have laid a golden egg at last, now I will be happy!"

The little brown hen asked the farmer's wife to place her wonderful golden egg in a window that overlooked the farmyard so that she could look at it whenever she wanted...and there it is to this day!

Lemon Is Locked Out

Joe and Kate had a new puppy. They named him Lemon because his fur was of the palest yellow.

Now, like all puppies, Lemon was very mischievous and very inquisitive. He liked to explore cardboard boxes and kitchen cupboards, but best of all he liked to play hide and seek near the fence at the bottom of the garden.

One day, Lemon found a loose board in the fence. Being an inquisitive little puppy, he poked his nose into the space and wriggled through to the street. Then away he went to explore the world outside. When he came back he couldn't find the loose board at all.

Someone had mended the hole in the fence and he was shut out. Lemon sat down and began to howl as loud as he could.

Joe and Kate heard him and came running to the fence. "You silly puppy!" they called. "Dad has mended the fence, but look, the garden gate is wide open!"

Lemon jumped up at once and wagging his stumpy little tail, he trotted in for tea!

34

Hoot's Big Secret

Hoot the tugboat worked in a busy harbour. All day, Hoot and the other tugboats guided the large ships along. Sometimes, they helped them stop in exactly the right place alongside the quay. Other times, the tugboats towed long lines of barges behind them from one part of the dock to the other, so that they could unload their cargos.

Now Hoot was the smallest of all the tugboats, but he was the strongest. He could pull the biggest of ships along by himself and needed no help from the other tugboats at all!

Now one day, the largest ship ever to come into the harbour was waiting outside. It was the tugboat's job to guide the great ship through the deepest water and enter the narrow harbour gates.

"It's far too big for us to move!" said one tugboat, as he stared up at the ship towering above him.

Then Hoot came racing across the harbour! All on his very own, he pulled the ship forward and it sailed though the gates with no bother at all.

"Hurray for Hoot!" the tugboats cheered. The big ship blew its great siren and all the boats in the harbour joined in. What a noise!

'How can a tiny tugboat pull such a great ship?' everyone wondered. Hoot knew the answer and so do you - but keep it a secret won't you!

Holly's Hide-out

Holly Hare hated gardening, it was hard work and far too messy! Sometimes, when the weather was warm, Holly sat in the flower garden and sunbathed, but she never set foot in the vegetable plot, just in case she might be asked to do something.

One day, as she was sitting outside reading, Holly suddenly felt very hungry. "I think, just this once, I shall stroll over to the vegetable plot and see what I can find!"

As there was no-one in sight, she picked a great armful of crisp lettuces, a big bunch of juicy carrots and an enormous cauliflower.

"I shall eat them all myself," giggled Holly. "I'll hide inside this little house where no-one will see me!"

Once inside, Holly quietly closed the door and began munching straight away.

As she tucked into her second carrot, Holly felt that someone was watching her. Slowly, she turned round and what do you think she saw? Every one of the Hare family watching her from behind the glass.

How the young hares laughed and how Holly blushed, especially when Father Hare gave her a spade and made her dig over the vegetable plot as a punishment for being so greedy!

Barnaby Goes Fishing

When Barnaby Bear felt like a lazy day, he always went fishing in Silver Lake.

He had his own special place by the lake shore and after he had been fishing for a while, he usually dozed off to sleep.

But today was different! "I feel full of energy this morning," said Barnaby, as he jogged along the shore, "the sun is hot and Silver Lake looks so inviting, I think I shall go for a swim!"

So Barnaby Bear took off his clothes and hung them carefully on a bush. Then he plunged into the clear waters of Silver Lake. He splashed around for over an hour until he began to feel very hungry.

"I'll get dried and dressed as quick as I can!" said Barnaby, thinking of the delicious food packed inside his picnic basket.

He stepped out of the water, shook his thick wet fur and looked around. "Where are my clothes?" he gasped. "I'm sure I left them on that bush over there!"

But the bush was quite empty, not so much as a sock in sight!

What had happened was, when Barnaby Bear hung up his clothes earlier, he hadn't noticed a moose in the bushes nibbling away. By accident Barnaby's clothes had got hooked upon the moose's antlers.

Poor old Barnaby, he'll probably have to go home wearing the picnic basket!

Evangeline Buys A Car

One day, Evangeline the china doll wanted to go shopping. "Bother!" she snapped as she looked out of the door, "it's raining and I shall get wet!"

"Never mind, I shall take you in my car!" It was the clown doll who lived next door.

"Don't bother!" said Evangeline, rather rudely. "Your car looks so silly. The doors drop off and the bonnet flies open, and people laugh when you drive down the street!"

The clown doll looked rather sad. He was very fond of Evangeline, although she was often horrid to him.

"I could walk to the shops with you and shelter you from the rain with my giant umbrella," said the clown doll very kindly.

"Alright," snapped Evangeline, "it's better than nothing!"

As the clown doll and Evangeline were walking towards town, they passed a car showroom.

"I've just had a wonderful idea!" shrieked Evangeline, clapping her hands. "I'll go inside and buy a brand new car. You can help me choose, clown doll!"

So, Evangeline marched into the showroom and in her loudest voice said, "I'll have the biggest car you have!"

The salesman looked very pleased and showed her the biggest and most expensive model in the showroom.

"I'll take it," said Evangeline very grandly.

"But Evangeline..." whispered the clown doll. "It won't..."

"Silence!" snapped Evangeline. "Drive this model home at once!"

As he drove home, the poor clown doll tried to speak, but Evangeline would not listen to a single word.

"I'm so proud of my flashy new car," sighed Evangeline, as she waved grandly to people they passed in the street.

At last, they reached home. "Park it in my garage," Evangeline ordered the clown doll with a wave of her hand.

"I can't do that!" replied the clown doll as he parked the car in the street outside. "Your new car is far too big for your garage, it's even too wide to go through your gate!"

"Oh dear me!" cried Evangeline, looking a bit ashamed. "I should have listened to you. You'll have to take my lovely car back."

"Why can't you take it back yourself?" asked the clown doll.

"Because I don't know how to drive!" whispered Evangeline, almost in tears.

How the clown doll laughed. "What a silly doll you are Evangeline! Before you buy another car, I will teach you to drive. Then we will choose one that will fit into your garage!"

Evangeline told the clown doll that she was sorry and learnt to drive in his funny circus car - even though parts did fall off sometimes!

Simon Takes Flight!

Once upon a time, there was a snail called Simon. All day long he was content just crawling slowly along the garden path. Sometimes, just for a change, he would crawl slowly up the garden wall - but this would take nearly all morning! Then, in the afternoon, he would slowly crawl down again!

Now Simon the snail was very happy with his way of life, but others around criticised.

All the birds and the bees, the mosquitoes, moths and insects that flew above him said, "Simon, you are so dull. You can't fly and you never see anything of the world but the garden wall and the path!"

Simon thought for a while, then he had to agree. "I wish I had wings and could see the world over the garden wall!"

Poor Simon felt so sad as he crawled away, he didn't even bother to look where he was going.

All of a sudden, the wind began to blow and Simon the snail was lifted up high above the garden. Higher and higher he flew until he was over the tops of the trees, almost as high as the clouds.

When Simon looked down in amazement, he could see fields and towns, mountains and rivers - he even glimpsed the bright blue sea. It was marvellous!

This is what had happened. A boy in the garden was flying his kite and as Simon crawled along, he landed on the tail and had been blown with the kite into the air.

"I can't wait to tell the others all about my adventure!" chuckled Simon, the flying snail, as he crawled slowly back down the garden path.

The Magical Snowmen

One wintery night an icy wind started to blow, then softly and silently, snow began to fall. As children in the Square awoke and looked out of their windows, everything was white. The gardens, the roads and the paths were all covered with a thick blanket of powdery, white snow.

As if by magic, all the front doors in the Square seemed to burst open at once! Out came children dressed in warm scarves, hats and boots all shrieking with delight. Dogs were rolling and barking in the snow, cats were howling to be let back inside with damp paws and wet whiskers.

The grown-ups however, were clearing up with every brush and shovel they could find. "Snow is such a nuisance!" they grumbled.

"Isn't it wonderful!" yelled the children.

All that day, the children played outside. They had the biggest snowball fight ever seen in the Square, and before darkness fell, each had built a snowman by their front gate.

That night, the children were so tired, they went to bed early and fell asleep straight away.

Now it may have been the town hall clock striking midnight that woke up all the children, or it may have been the moon shining bright on the snow covered Square, but one by one every single boy and girl woke up, got out of bed and looked out of the window. You'll never guess what they saw!

Down in the Square below, their snowmen were having a wonderful time. Some were shaking hands and hugging one another, some were dancing up and down or sliding on the slippery paths. How the children stared when their snowmen all joined in a splendid snowball fight in the moonlight!

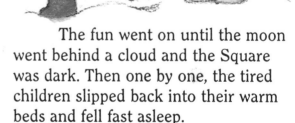

The fun went on until the moon went behind a cloud and the Square was dark. Then one by one, the tired children slipped back into their warm beds and fell fast asleep.

Next morning, when the children woke up, they all rushed over to their windows, drew back the curtains and looked into the Square.

There they saw the snowmen standing perfectly still by each front gate. Perhaps it had been a dream after all...but if the children had looked even more closely that snowy winter's morning, they may have noticed that all their snowmen had in fact changed places in the night!

45

Rescue On The Bridge

It had seemed a very long week for the Yellow Rescue Helicopter. He had made no rescues at all! Not one single person had floated out of their depth at sea on an air bed. No-one had been stranded on the rocks as the tide came in, and nobody had fallen down the cliffs and needed help.

The Yellow Rescue Helicopter was bored! "I've not moved from this spot for a whole week," he moaned. "I will soon forget how to fly and my blades might get rusty!"

Then all of a sudden the emergency bell rang, the sirens howled and the rescue pilot came running across the airfield.

He started the blades up at once and shouted above the noise, "We're needed urgently! Fly as fast as you can to the bridge over the bay!"

The Yellow Rescue Helicopter took off at once and was soon swooping low over the water. The pilot guided him under the bridge, then swept up over the top.

As he gazed below, the Yellow Rescue Helicopter could see no-one in the water and no boats in trouble at all.

"Look down there," shouted the pilot, "the bridge is blocked!"

Two gigantic lorries crossing the bridge had broken down. No traffic could cross and the lorries were far too big to be towed away.

"Can you fly close to the bridge, just above one the lorries?" yelled the pilot.

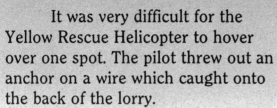

It was very difficult for the Yellow Rescue Helicopter to hover over one spot. The pilot threw out an anchor on a wire which caught onto the back of the lorry.

Very, very carefully, the Yellow Rescue Helicopter flew backwards and dragged the lorry clear of the bridge.

The pilot cheered. "Well done! Now we must fly back and move the other one too!"

The second lorry was even bigger. It took every bit of the Yellow Rescue Helicopter's power to pull the lorry across, but at last they reached the end of the bridge.

Very soon the traffic was speeding across once again. All the drivers honked their horns to thank the Yellow Rescue Helicopter and the pilot as they drove past.

"Well done!" said the pilot, as he flew back to base. "I think that's enough excitement for today." And the Yellow Rescue Helicopter agreed!

Leonard, The Bold, Brave Lion

"I'm bold, brave and fearless!" shouted Leonard the lion to all of his friends.

"Of course you are," they sighed because they had all heard Leonard boasting many times before.

One day when they were walking in the forest listening to Leonard boasting as usual, they turned a corner and saw a castle. On the gate outside was a notice that read, *One Castle For Sale*.

"That's just the right place for me!" cried Leonard. "A bold, brave and fearless lion should live in a castle, then I will be King of the Castle!"

"It looks a bit spooky to me," said one of his friends. "Won't you be frightened when darkness comes?"

"Don't be ridiculous!" snapped Leonard. "I am a bold, brave and fearless lion!"

So Leonard bought the castle at once and moved in the very next day. All his friends came round to help. It was very hard work moving Leonard's heavy furniture up the winding stone staircase.

At last, everything was unpacked and in place. Leonard's friends waved goodbye and set off for home.

Now, the rest of that day Leonard was so busy marching around shouting, "I'm the King of the Castle!" that he forgot to look where the light switches were. So that night, when it grew dark he couldn't find his way!

He crept round the room trying to find the door, then he groped along the wall feeling for the light switch.

"Oh dear," Leonard trembled. "It's very spooky all alone in the dark."

Then all at once a door creaked open and something brushed across Leonard's nose.

"It's a ghost!" he screamed. "Perhaps it's a bat, or a witch, or a skeleton or maybe it's a lion-eating monster!"

Poor Leonard began to shake and quiver and quake all over from head to toe. Then he stretched out a paw and touched something slimey, he turned round and felt something nudge against him.

"Help! Help!" cried Leonard, in a squeaky voice. "I wish I really was bold, brave and fearless."

Just then the door opened and the light was switched on, and there stood all Leonard's friends.

"Why are you standing in the dark?" asked one.

"Haven't you noticed our special surprise?" said another.

Leonard looked around the room. The table was set for a party, with a big iced cake and lots of party food.

"I thought the room was full of monsters and ghosts," whispered Leonard, still trembling.

"Here are your ghosts!" said one friend, and he pointed to the streamers and balloons that had brushed Leonard's nose and nudged him in the dark.

"And here is your slimey monster!" laughed another, as he stuck a spoon in a big jelly on the table.

"We got the party ready this afternoon," the friends explained. "Then we came back tonight to join in the fun."

Leonard looked very relieved. "I am a silly lion," he grinned. "I've had such a fright and it's all my own fault!"

His friends gathered round to listen. "I'm not really a bold, brave, fearless lion at all," he said, and everybody smiled. "This castle is so big, I would like you all to come and live here with me."

All his friends thought that this was a wonderful idea and agreed at once.

"There's just one more thing," said Leonard, as he tucked in to a giant slice of cake. "Could you all stay here tonight?...just to keep me company!"

Miss Mole Baby-sits

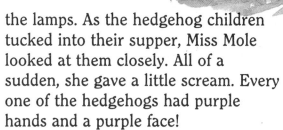

One morning Mrs Hedgehog received a letter in the mail. It was an invitation to go out to supper.

"I really would like to go," sighed Mrs Hedgehog as she read the invitation out loud, "but who will look after my ten little hedgehogs?"

Now Miss Mole, who was scurrying by to fetch her morning newspaper, overheard Mrs Hedgehog as she stood on her doorstep. "I'd love to baby-sit for you," offered Miss Mole. "I'm very fond of your ten children, and they know me very well."

So that was settled. The very next evening, at seven o'clock on the dot, Mrs Hedgehog went out to supper in her very best dress. And a very excited Miss Mole took charge of ten little hedgehogs.

"Can we go out to play in the woods for a while?" the eldest hedgehog asked Miss Mole.

"Of course you can, but remember to come back as soon as it begins to get dark."

The ten little hedgehogs were very good and as soon as the sun sank behind the hill, they came home at once.

As they came through the front door, Miss Mole counted each one. There were ten little hedgehogs all safe and sound. Miss Mole sighed with relief. "Come into the kitchen and eat your supper, but first wash your hands and faces!"

Miss Mole busied about the kitchen setting the table and lighting the lamps. As the hedgehog children tucked into their supper, Miss Mole looked at them closely. All of a sudden, she gave a little scream. Every one of the hedgehogs had purple hands and a purple face!

"We've been picking blackberries!" piped up Baby Hedgehog, "and these are for you." From under the table two of the children lifted up a huge basket of juicy blackberries.

"How very kind," said Miss Mole with a gasp, "but how on earth am I going to get you clean before your mother comes home?"

As soon as the little hedgehogs had gobbled up their supper, Miss Mole hurried them into the bathroom. But however hard she rubbed and scrubbed with soap and brushes, not one bit of purple dye came off the ten little hedgehogs.

"Oh dear!" cried Miss Mole quite worn out. "Whatever shall I do?"

"I know," laughed Baby Hedgehog, and from the bathroom cupboard he pulled a big bottle of bubble bath.

Straight away, Miss Mole turned on the taps, filled up the bath and all the little hedgehogs jumped in.

What a time they had! There were bubbles everywhere and quite a few puddles on the bathroom floor as well. After a long soak everyone was clean, and every trace of the purple had disappeared completely.

The ten little hedgehogs were tired out, so they went to bed and fell fast asleep - and so did Miss Mole!

Bobby Rabbit And Mr. Fox

Bobby Rabbit was very lazy. He hated cleaning his house. He hated washing up, but most of all he hated drawing water from the well. As he filled up the buckets, he muttered to himself, "This is too big and the water is too heavy. This is no job for a clever rabbit like me!"

Now Mr. Fox, who was hiding round the back of the house overheard Bobby Rabbit. He smiled slyly to himself, thought for a while, then came up with a cunning plan.

The very next day, when Bobby Rabbit was drawing water from the well, Mr. Fox paid him a visit.

"Good morning Bobby Rabbit!" called Mr. Fox, as he strode down the garden path carrying a cardboard box. "No more heaving buckets of water for you. I have the perfect answer to all your problems!"

Bobby Rabbit put down his buckets and rushed over to look in the fox's box.

"Taps!" cried Bobby holding up two shiny, silver taps. "Why didn't I think of that?"

So straight away he paid Mr. Fox all the money in his money box and thanked him for his trouble.

"I shall never have to fill another bucket as long as I live!" chuckled Bobby, as he nailed the two taps to the wall above his kitchen sink. "I'll boil the kettle and make myself a pot of tea!" He turned on the cold water tap. Nothing happened! So, he turned on the hot water tap. Still nothing happened, not one drop of water!

Bobby looked underneath, he poked his fingers into the holes, he even banged the taps with a hammer. Still nothing happened!

Aunt May, who was passing by, called in to find out what all the banging was about.

"I bought these taps and they don't work!" snapped Bobby, very cross indeed.

Aunt May laughed. "You'll have to fetch water from the well for a while longer, you silly rabbit! You must ask a plumber to connect your taps to the main water supply before any water will flow through!"

Bobby Rabbit looked upset. "I've been tricked by that sly old fox!"

"I'm afraid you have!" giggled Aunt May. "Now go and get a bucket of water from the well and we'll both have a cup of tea!"

Ogden and The Dinosaur

For the first time in his life, Ogden had a bedroom all to himself. Ogden's room had new curtains, carpet, new drawers and a wardrobe, but the thing Ogden liked best of all was his new bed cover.

It was soft and warm, as you would expect, but instead of flowers or a pretty pattern, it had a green dinosaur right in the middle and a yellow border round the edge.

"What a great cover!" said Ogden, as he threw himself down on the bed.

"Watch where you're putting your elbows!" said a voice.

Before Ogden could reply, there was a green dinosaur standing on his new carpet, and the bed cover was quite empty - except for the yellow border round the edge!

"What are our plans for today?" the dinosaur asked Ogden eagerly.

"You're a dinosaur!" gasped Ogden, with his mouth wide open. "I have a green dinosaur in my new bedroom!"

The dinosaur pushed open the bedroom door. "Jump up and we'll go for a ride!"

Ogden rode his green dinosaur down the drive, out of the gate and down the lane. They went on through the wood, up the hill, stopped a while at the top, then back down again.

"What do you eat?" Ogden asked his new friend. "Not people, I hope!"

"No, I prefer green things, like apples and cress, and I love sprouting broccoli and kale!" said the dinosaur.

"Would a cauliflower do?" Ogden asked as they rode past a vegetable stall.

"A boxful would be nice," said the dinosaur licking his lips, "and a few lettuce to finish with!"

Ogden rode back on his dinosaur and waved to everyone he knew. "A green dinosaur! How exciting!" they all said.

When they went upstairs, Ogden threw himself on the bed. He stared at the bed cover and there was the green dinosaur back in the middle. But Ogden was sure he heard a voice say, "See you tomorrow!"

Mildred Moves House

Mildred the country mouse thought it was about time she moved house. "It's getting far too busy near this road and sometimes it can be quite dangerous!" she told her children. "My cousin has sent word that there is a fallen tree to rent near her," she went on, "it's in a quiet lane and sounds like a perfect place for our new home!"

The four little mice could hardly wait to pack up and move on, for they had always wanted to live in a tree, full of secret passages and hiding places.

Mildred's neighbours made her and her family feel very welcome. They brought baskets full of tasty treats to eat, honey flavoured drinks and a chocolate drop or two for each of the children.

"Is there anything at all you need for your new home?" Mildred's cousin asked kindly.

"Indeed there is," Mildred replied. "I would like some nutshells!"

Now wasn't that a strange request!

Nevertheless, two of the strongest mice fetched a bag full of nutshells and emptied them out on the floor in front of Mildred.

"Oh my goodness!" she cried. "These are no good, they're broken into little pieces!"

The Grumpy Teddy Bears

People came every day to look in the window, but no-one came inside the shop to buy. Grandpa Button felt very disappointed.

Along a certain street in Toy Village is a very special shop which sells all kinds of teddy bears. Children come from far and wide to choose the bears and take them home to love them forever.

But it wasn't always so! Many years ago, Grandpa Button spent all day long making teddies, but he never sold a single one.

His shop window was always full of bears in all colours and sizes. There were honey coloured bears with black stitched noses, golden teddies with soft suede paws, white bears, black bears and cuddly brown ones that growled when you gave them a squeeze.

Then one day, Grandpa Button's cousin Emily paid a visit to Toy Village. As she passed the shop window, she looked at all the teddies and gave a little scream.

Grandpa Button put down his work and rushed outside.

"Look at all the teddies' faces!" cried cousin Emily, pointing at the window. "You've stitched their smiles on upside down. No wonder no-one buys the poor things, they all look so grumpy!" Grandpa Button had to agree.

"We can soon change all that," said cousin Emily, as she came inside and took off her coat. Straight away, she pulled out her sewing kit, and with her needle and thread she soon stitched happy smiles onto every teddy bear.

It wasn't very long before all the teddy bears in the window were sold. Cousin Emily couldn't refuse staying with Grandpa Button and helping him make hundreds more teddies for children everywhere to love!

Fizzy Grizzly

Fizzy Grizzly lived in a forest park. He was a very friendly grizzly bear and liked to wander along the paths and tracks to meet the hikers and backpackers, and talk to the folks camping and walking in the forest.

Sometimes he would give them quite a shock as he popped out from behind the trees, but Fizzy Grizzly would shake hands and offer to show them the way. He would even help to put up their tents and build camp fires.

Soon the visitors got to know Fizzy. He made lots of new friends and went to picnics and barbecues every single day!

Now perhaps you may be wondering how a grizzly bear got such a strange name!

Visitors to the park called him Fizzy because he loved fizzy drinks! In cans, or bottles, or from a glass with a straw - Fizzy loved them all!

He drank so many fizzy drinks, he often had the hiccups. You could hear Fizzy all over the park. Hic! Hic! Hic! All day long!

In the evening, Fizzy would sit round the campers' fires and drink a whole boxful of fizzy drinks. Then he would hiccup all the way home through the forest in the moonlight, waking up the other animals as he passed by. Hic! Hic! Hic!

Now when the first few flakes of snow began to fall in the park, it meant that winter was on the way. Then Fizzy Grizzly would say goodbye to his friends and go home to hibernate until spring.

Fizzy Grizzly enjoyed his long winter sleep, snug and warm in his bed, when the world outside was frozen and cold. But sad to say, no-one else did!

Fizzy Grizzly had been drinking fizzy drinks all summer long, so he hiccuped loudly until he woke up in the spring.

Hic! Hic! Hic! Fizzy Grizzly slept peacefully. Hic! Hic! Hic! Everyone else was wide awake!

The Bad-tempered Spinning Top

Once upon a time there was a brightly coloured spinning top. He lived with the rest of the toys on a little girl's bedroom floor.

Now the spinning top was a bad-tempered fellow, he liked his own way and could be quite horrid at times. Some days when he was in a bad mood, he would whizz round and round the bedroom floor spinning on the toys' toes, or pushing them hard against the wall.

"Get out of the way, you stupid things!" he hummed, as he flew round the room. "I need more space than you!"

The toys got out of the way as fast as they could, for a top on your toes can be quite painful.

Now one day, the top made up his mind to take a look at the world outside, so he spun out of the house and down the street without even saying goodbye.

As the top whirled along, he spotted a large playground. "What a perfect place for me to spin!" cried the top, and with that he shot through the gate and began to whizz round and round.

All of a sudden, something hit the top and he went hurtling across the playground. He only just managed to stay upright and keep spinning!

Then without any warning, something else crashed into him. The poor top flew up into the air and landed upside down, still spinning! Then he felt another bang and another. Bang! Crash! Wallop! He stopped spinning at once and took a look around.

There in the playground were four boys practising on skateboards. The top had been far too busy whirling round to notice them. The boys were having a wonderful time on their skateboards and they didn't see the top at all!

"Now I know what the toys feel like when I spin on their toes," said the top rather sadly.

He went back home and said he was very sorry to the toys...and sometimes, but only if he is asked, the top will give a special spinning display to tunes played by the toy music box!

Ready Teddy's Big Adventure

When Teddy was invited to parties he would choose an extra special costume. It took him simply ages to get dressed, and when his friends came to call they would shout, "Are you ready Teddy?" But Teddy never was, so his friends called him 'Ready Teddy'!

Once upon a time, there was a Teddy Bear who loved to dress up the street where he lived was a costume shop, so Teddy could borrow a different set of clothes every day.

Sometimes he would be a cowboy or an Indian chief, another day he would dress as a pirate or a wizard.

Once when Ready Teddy was dressed as a racing driver, he was asked to take part in a race. Then to Ready Teddy's great surprise, he came in first and won the prize!

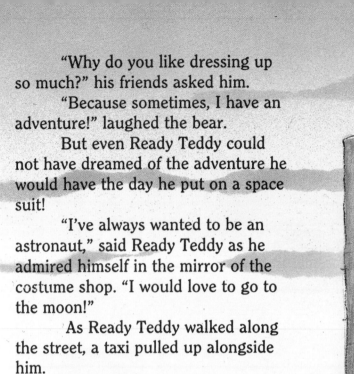

"Why do you like dressing up so much?" his friends asked him.

"Because sometimes, I have an adventure!" laughed the bear.

But even Ready Teddy could not have dreamed of the adventure he would have the day he put on a space suit!

"I've always wanted to be an astronaut," said Ready Teddy as he admired himself in the mirror of the costume shop. "I would love to go to the moon!"

As Ready Teddy walked along the street, a taxi pulled up alongside him.

"Can I take you to the launching pad?" said the driver, so Ready Teddy jumped inside.

When the taxi stopped, he could hardly believe his eyes, for there, waiting to be launched, was an enormous silver rocket.

"I think I'll take a look inside," said Ready Teddy, climbing up the launching ramp.

The door at the very top of the rocket was open, and that is where Ready Teddy's adventure began.

Before he knew what was happening, the rocket was launched on its journey through space with Ready Teddy at the controls.

At last it landed on the moon and Ready Teddy, in his astronaut's suit, got out, took a look around, then went for a ride in a moon buggy.

"I'd better hoist a flag, just to show I've been here!" said Ready Teddy proudly. And after that, he took a last look around and got back into his rocket.

At the end of a long journey, Ready Teddy splashed down safely in the sea. A boat picked him up and took him to shore where the taxi was waiting.

"Take me back to the costume shop please!" Ready Teddy told the taxi driver.

"I'm going to choose another costume, and maybe I shall have another adventure as exciting as this one!"

Woolly Rabbit Gets Wet

One summer night, Woolly Rabbit was left outside in the garden. He was rather small, so when the children collected up their toys, they must have missed him.

That night, it rained and rained. The rag doll, who was very fond of the rabbit, was so worried, she almost cried!

The next day the children's puppy found Woolly Rabbit under a bush. His fur was wet and soggy and he looked very sorry for himself.

The children squeezed the water out of their rabbit, then hung him on the washing line to dry. Woolly Rabbit didn't like that one bit!

At last, he was fluffy and dry and put back with the other toys. The rag doll was overjoyed to see him return safe and sound.

"This must never happen again!" she said hugging Woolly Rabbit very tightly.

So she found a red ribbon from the sewing box and tied it in a big bow around the rabbit's neck. On the end of the ribbon, she sewed a little silver bell left over from Christmas.

"Now you'll never get left outside again!" she smiled, and gave Woolly Rabbit a great big hug!

69

Ten Noisy Little Hedgehogs

When all the ten little hedgehogs were at school, Mrs Hedgehog would often remark how peaceful and quiet the house was! But when they returned at four o'clock, it could get a little noisy!

One day, when the hedgehogs came home they were very excited. As they ran through the door, each one was carrying a musical instrument.

"We are learning to play tunes together," said the eldest. "Let's play you one now!"

So Mrs Hedgehog sat down in her chair to listen.

The ten little hedgehogs stood in a group, opened their music books, took a deep breath and began to play.

"Oh my goodness," gasped Mrs Hedgehog as she sat up in her chair, "what a dreadful noise!"

The ten little hedgehogs played on and on and the music got worse and worse. At last they stopped and Baby Hedgehog climbed up onto his mother's knee. "I think we need to practise!" he said with a grin.

Night after night, the little hedgehogs played their music together, but however hard they practised, they never sounded any better. Poor Mrs Hedgehog got no peace at all!

Now one morning, while the little hedgehogs were at school, Mrs Hedgehog sat quietly reading a magazine. Suddenly, she spied an advertisement on the very last page. When she read it, she jumped up from her chair with glee, for this was the very thing she had been looking for!

A few days later the postman delivered a long flat box to Mrs Hedgehog and when the children came home at four o'clock, they found a surprise waiting for them.

It was a xylophone! The notes sounded soft and melodic, and everyone could play together - even Baby Hedgehog!

Soon the children were playing beautiful tunes and all their woodland neighbours came regularly to listen.

Edward The Flying Elephant

Do you believe that elephants can fly? Edward can! He flies high in the sky above the clouds then dives down low, almost touching the ground. Sometimes he loops the loop or flies upside down, which gives his passengers a fright!

One day, while Edward was checking his plane, he heard a message on his radio:

Two explorers are missing in the Great Rainforest. Can anyone help?

Straight away, Edward jumped into his plane and took off. "I'll fly over the Great Rainforest and see if I can find them before it gets dark!"

It didn't take Edward long to spot the two explorers as he dived down low over the trees. They were paddling their canoe down the river which wound through the dense forest.

"No wonder they're lost," said Edward out loud. "They're going the wrong way! There's nowhere for me to land, so how can I tell them to head back?"

All of a sudden, Edward had a brilliant idea! Quickly he turned his plane round and flew high up into the sky. He looped the loop a couple of times then made a directing arrow with smoke from his plane.

The two explorers saw it straight away and understood what it meant. They turned their canoe round and in next to no time had paddled back up the river and returned safe and sound.

Wasn't it lucky for them that elephants really can fly!

Yellow Feather Goes Hunting

Once upon a time, there was a little Indian boy called Yellow Feather. He lived at the bottom of a wide canyon.

One day, his father gave him his very own bow and lots of tiny arrows. Little Yellow Feather felt very proud, and every night, he dreamed he was a great hunter.

"Hear me, all you creatures!" shouted Yellow Feather. "Flee for your lives, for here comes the greatest hunter in the whole valley!" The little Indian's voice echoed round the rocks as he ran through the hot, dusty canyon.

All of a sudden, Yellow Feather spied a lizard lying by a rock. "Go away little boy and don't point that arrow at me!" yawned the lizard and went back to sleep in the hot sun.

Next Yellow Feather spotted an armadillo scurrying across the path. He took aim straight away!

"Stop playing games with that bow and arrow. It's far too hot!" said the armadillo and with that he rolled himself into a ball and went to sleep too!

Then all of a sudden, a roadrunner sped by and Yellow Feather ran after him as fast as he could.

With the speed of lightning, the roadrunner ran through the canyon and into the desert. Then he ran round and round the cactus until he made little Yellow Feather feel quite dizzy.

"Can't catch me with your bow and arrow!" squealed the roadrunner. Then he disappeared in cloud of dust.

Little Yellow Feather sat on the ground. "I'm lost and a long way from home," he said, trying hard not to cry. "Whatever shall I do?"

Just then, a friendly coyote came by. He could see that Yellow Feather was alone and needed someone to help him.

So the coyote scrambled up onto a flat rock, sat down and lifted back his head and gave his wildest coyote howl. The sound could be heard right to the edge of the wide canyon. Then another coyote took up the howl, then another and another, all the way down the canyon until Yellow Feather's father heard the call.

At once, he understood what was wrong. He jumped on his fastest horse and galloped off to find little Yellow Feather.

The coyote's calls guided him far into the canyon, where he found his son sitting by the side of his new friend the coyote...who was still howling!

The Runaway Toys

Once upon a time, there was an old toy maker who made clockwork toys. People came from near and far to buy them and to watch them all whirring around in his tiny shop.

Sometimes, the toy maker made clockwork mice that darted all over the floor. Sometimes, he made birds that hopped across the table. He even made a set of false teeth that rattled and snapped as they spun round and round!

The clockwork toys worked so well, they would whizz all over the place. But some got lost behind cupboards and others walked off the window ledge onto the roof below, where the old toy maker couldn't reach them.

One day, a visitor to the shop solved the problem. Out of his coat pocket he pulled a huge magnet. He tied one end of a piece of string to a long stick and the other round the magnet.

Soon he was collecting up all the lost toys that were out of reach. The old man was delighted and spent all that day playing with the runaway toys!

Lucy's Lunch

It was almost lunch-time and Lucy the long-legged goose was feeling rather hungry. "I wish the farmer's wife would hurry up and feed us!" said Lucy impatiently. "I think I will go and find out where she is!"

So straight away Lucy dashed over to the farmhouse and peeped through the window. Inside was the farmer's wife making lunch for the farmer.

As Lucy the goose looked into the kitchen she could hardly believe her eyes. "My favourite!" smiled Lucy. "Lots and lots of big fat juicy long wriggling worms!"

And with that she ran back to the farmyard to tell the others what a treat was in store for them at lunch-time.

At last, the farmer's wife opened her kitchen door and scattered handfuls of corn into the farmyard as usual.

"Where are all those lovely juicy worms I saw you cooking on the kitchen stove earlier?" cried Lucy.

Just then the farmer came round the corner. "That's my favourite lunch Lucy!" he said with a grin. "Spaghetti in tomato sauce - not worms!"

Everybody in the farmyard fell about laughing. That was, except for Lucy the long-legged goose, who felt rather silly!

The Mischievous Fox Cub

Rusty the fox cub was always up to mischief. Whenever he went out to play, his mother would say, "Rusty, try not to get into any mischief and don't poke your nose into other people's business!" But Rusty did - all the time! He just couldn't help himself!

One day, the mischievous little fox cub went to take a look at Mrs Swan sitting on her eggs by the river bank. Now swans can be fierce, but Rusty didn't know that and almost lost his tail!

Another time when he was passing the farmyard gate, he decided to pop inside, just to find out where Mr Turkey lived. Now Rusty didn't know that turkeys do not like foxes, not even little ones. This time Rusty got a sharp peck on the nose - and he was only trying to be friendly!

"Oh dear!" said Rusty to himself, as he trotted through the wood. "I really must try not to get into any more mischief!"

Just then, he heard a rustling in the undergrowth. "I'll just find out what made that noise," he said, sticking his nose into a pile of dry leaves.

"Ouch!" Rusty yelped, as he jumped back. Something had pricked him right on the nose and it really hurt.

"Sorry!" said a tiny voice. Then out from under the leaves came a little hedgehog. "Didn't your mother ever tell you not to poke your nose into other people's business?" giggled the prickly little hedgehog. Rusty had to laugh too!

Snowy The Seagull

Snowy the seagull loved the lifeboat. Everyday he would watch from the cliff top, just in case it was launched into the sea below. "I don't think I shall be lucky today," said Snowy with a sigh. "The sea is so calm and still, nobody will need the lifeboat!"

So, he flew off to join the other gulls on top of the rocks...but the gulls were not alone, sitting on top of the rocks were three children looking very frightened.

"We came to take photographs of the gulls and our boat has floated away!" said one of them.

"The water is rising very fast," said another. "What shall we do?"

"Don't worry!" called Snowy, as he flew away. "I'll bring help!" Then the seagull flew across the water straight to the lifeboat station.

At once, the crew launched the lifeboat. "Fly above us," called the Captain to Snowy, "and show us the way to the rocks as fast as you can."

All of a sudden, a strong wind began to blow and storm clouds gathered. The lifeboat started to toss about in the huge waves.

"Can you see those rocks?" the Captain shouted to Snowy above the noise of the gale.

Just at that moment the seagull saw the children. Now there was only one tiny piece of rock left for them to cling to. Snowy flew down and landed beside them. "Hang on!" said the gull. "Help is on the way!"

At last, the lifeboat came into view and the crew rescued the children. Soon they were all back at the lifeboat station, safe and dry.

"You're quite a hero. Snowy!" laughed the Captain. "I think you ought to join our crew, then you could keep a look out for anyone in trouble on the rocks. Well done, Snowy, lookout for the lifeboat!"

The Turtle's Slippery Slide

One winter's day, it was frosty and cold and everywhere was white with snow. It was a perfect day for climbing up the nearest hill and sliding down to the bottom.

Everyone was searching their garages and looking in lofts for sledges and toboggans.

"Race you up to the top of the hill!" yelled one of the bears, who was carrying an old tin bath.

"Race you down to the bottom!" shouted another, perched on a big wooden tray.

Then everybody slid down the hill all at once. Two on a toboggan, three sharing a sledge, all skimming and sliding down the slippery slope to land in soft piles of snow at the bottom.

It was such wonderful fun whizzing down the hill and trudging back up again, especially for the little green turtle. He didn't need a toboggan, or a sledge, or a tin bath, or a tray. In fact, he didn't need anything at all!

The Flying Display

Gerry the pilot felt very proud. He had been chosen to be the leader in the flying display at the air show in one week's time.

"Wonderful!" exclaimed Gerry, and rushed across the airfield to tell the other pilots. Now because he was so excited, or perhaps he just didn't look where he was going, Gerry tripped, fell flat on his face and sprained his ankle!

"Sorry," said the doctor, who looked at Gerry's leg. "No more flying for two whole weeks!"

Poor Gerry, he looked so disappointed.

On the afternoon of the flying display, Gerry sat outside the control tower looking very glum indeed.

Although he couldn't take part, his pilot friends made sure that he cheered up and enjoyed the show!

The Twins Keep Busy

Aunt Janet had asked the twins to come and stay with her lots of times, but Meg and Martin always had an excuse.

"We really don't want to go!" the twins told their mother. "There's nothing to do at Aunt Janet's and it will be very boring!"

"Go and stay for just one night," said Mother with a little smile. "You may be surprised!"

So one weekend, when Meg and Martin couldn't think of any more excuses, they went off to Aunt Janet's for the night.

"I'm afraid I haven't any toys for you to play with," said their aunt, as she opened the door to the twins. "But there's plenty to keep you amused in the kitchen!"

"I hope she doesn't want us to cook or wash up!" Martin whispered.

"Sssh," replied Meg, as she stepped inside. "She'll hear you!"

Aunt Janet's kitchen was huge with a large pine table full of all kinds of things.

"Hey!" cried Martin as he sat down. "Face paints and glue. Look, there's plaster and clay, there's even papier maché!"

84

"Make as much mess as you like," Aunt Janet laughed. "I'll join you and make a mess too!"

The twins soon found that Aunt Janet was brilliant at making models and kites, all kinds of costumes and very scary masks.

She could make paper dolls that stretched across the room, and trees from rolled up newspaper that almost reached the ceiling.

The hours passed so quickly it was soon time for bed.

"Don't bother clearing up the mess," called Aunt Janet as she made the supper. "We'll make a lot more tomorrow!"

Next morning they had breakfast in a tree house that Aunt Janet had put up a few years ago. By lunch-time, they knew how to make stilts from tin cans, read a compass and build a puppet theatre from a cardboard box.

Aunt Janet showed them how to cook quick home-made pizzas with frothy milkshakes, and chocolate crunchies for lunch.

Would you believe that the twins stayed with Aunt Janet a whole week, there was so much to do!

When they went home at last, it took ages to tell their mother about all the things they had done.

"I know!" she said with a grin. "I did exactly the same when we used to play together as children!"

Ogden's Rainy Day

Ogden had a new bed cover with a green dinosaur design right in the middle. Whenever he closed his eyes tight and threw himself down on the cover, there was a green dinosaur standing on his new bedroom carpet!

"What are we going to do today?" the dinosaur asked Ogden as he trundled across to the window.

"Look outside," Ogden sighed. "It's pouring with rain, so we shall have to stay indoors."

"Not a bit of it!" snorted the dinosaur. "I've never been outside in the rain before, so let's get moving!"

"You'll get very wet!" grinned Ogden, pulling on his coat and boots.

"Never mind," giggled the dinosaur. "I'm waterproof!"

Once the green dinosaur was outside, the fun began. His enormous feet splashed through the puddles and wet Ogden and his friends from top to toe. His giant tail swished from side to side spraying water over everyone.

"Isn't rain wonderful!" shouted the dinosaur.

"It is if you're waterproof!" Ogden yelled back, dripping wet.

The green dinosaur was enjoying himself so much that he forgot where he was putting his big feet. He travelled over the wet grass, on through the flower beds and was soon covered in thick sticky mud. When he swished his tail from left to right, mud flew everywhere, and this made matters even worse.

"How are we going to get you clean?" gasped poor Ogden. "I've never seen so much mud!"

"Don't worry," laughed the dinosaur. "I think it looks good!"

But Ogden was thinking about his new bedroom carpet when they got back to the house.

As Ogden and his friends hurried home in the rain with a very dirty dinosaur, they passed a garage.

In one corner of the forecourt was just the thing they needed - a car wash!

Ogden pressed a coin into the machine and very soon the dinosaur was clean and sparkling once more.

"Did you enjoy going out in the rain?" Ogden asked the green dinosaur when they got back to his bedroom. But as Ogden threw himself onto the bed, he stared at the bed cover - and there was the green dinosaur back in the middle once again!

Tim's New Soap

Tim loved playing with water, but he hated getting washed! He hated washing behind his ears and the back of his neck, but most of all he hated washing his face.

The rest of Tim's family loved getting washed and spent hours in the bathroom. Tim found this very strange indeed!

Now one day, when Tim was out shopping, he bought some trick soap from the joke shop. Tim read the label, *Guaranteed to turn your hands and face red when you get washed!* What fun he would have with that!

"I'll leave it on the wash basin," sniggered Tim, "and wait to see what happens!"

Mother used the bathroom first, but she had a shower and used her own shower gel.

Sister Sue took hours in the bathroom, but she used the perfumed soap her boyfriend had given her. Tim could smell it all over the house.

No-one used the trick soap at all and Tim went off to bed that night rather disappointed.

Next morning, Tim overslept. "Hurry up!" called Mother up the stairs. "Get washed and dressed as quickly as you can, or you will miss the school bus."

Tim jumped out of bed, grabbed his clothes and ran into the bathroom. He filled the basin with hot water, reached for the soap and washed himself at double speed. Quickly, he ran downstairs getting dressed as he went.

"You've just time for some breakfast!" called his mother from the kitchen.

But dear oh dear, as Tim sat down at the kitchen table, the whole family burst out laughing.

"What have you done to your face and hands?" asked Father, laughing so much he almost choked on his toast!

"Look in the mirror!" Sue shrieked, pointing at him.

Tim looked at himself and then he remembered. He had picked up the trick soap by mistake, his face was all red and so were his hands. The joke was on him!

The trick soap took ages to wash off. Tim was late for school and had to explain to his teacher - and she laughed loudest of all!

Take Me For A Ride

Robin liked cars. He had a box full of model cars that he played with everyday. He loved trips out in his father's car and never got bored however long the journey.

"I wish I could drive a car," said Robin to his father one day as they were driving along.

"I'm afraid you'll have to wait a long time before you can learn," his father laughed. "In the mean time, you'll have to be a passenger!"

Now on his next birthday, Robin was given a pedal car as a present. He thought it was wonderful and drove it everyday.

"How do you like driving?" joked his father, as the little boy raced up and down the path in his new car.

"It's great," Robin replied, "but I wish I had a passenger to ride around with me."

"I don't think your car is quite big enough," laughed Daddy. "You'll have to wait a few years until you can drive a real car, then you'll have plenty of passengers."

But Robin didn't have to wait *that* long. He looked outside and found a passenger waiting to be taken for a ride straight away!

The Great Green Caterpillar

One warm afternoon, a tiny brown sparrow was splashing around in the birdbath in the middle of the lawn. All of a sudden, he glanced down and saw the biggest caterpillar you can ever imagine moving along the garden path.

Straight away, he flew up into the apple tree and told the magpie. "It's almost as long as a snake!" chirped the tiny sparrow, "with lots and lots of bright green legs!"

The magpie flapped his wings. "I love caterpillars, especially big and juicy bright green ones. I shall have it for my tea!"

Now the woodpecker on the branch above heard him and said, "That enormous caterpillar will be far too big for you. I shall fly down and help you gobble it up!"

So, the birds flew out of the tree and landed right next to the giant caterpillar.

"Nobody is going to eat us!" croaked lots of little voices that seemed to be coming from the caterpillar.

The startled magpie and the woodpecker fell over backwards with fright.

You see the giant caterpillar was made up of lots and lots of green frogs. "This costume for the lakeside party this afternoon certainly fooled you two greedy birds!" giggled the cheeky frogs.

Creepy Crawler

There was once a gigantic tractor that ran on tracks, not wheels. Now this tractor was very strong, but very, very slow. He crawled along, moving heavy logs through the forest, no faster than a snail. So that is why the lumberjacks called him Creepy Crawler!

Moving the trunks of great pine trees was very hard work. As soon as the lumberjacks had cut them down, Creepy Crawler and his driver would carefully drag the logs to the sawmill to be cut into pieces.

Creepy Crawler and his driver worked all day long and in all kinds of weather.

"You're the strongest tractor in the whole forest!" the driver told Creepy Crawler as they drove through the tall pine trees. "That is why you have been chosen to do a very special job today!"

"How exciting," said Creepy Crawler. "I shall do my very best!"

When they reached the middle of the forest, the lumberjacks were busy cutting down the biggest pine tree of all, it's branches almost reached the sky.

At last, it toppled to the ground, just missing Creepy Crawler's bonnet!

Very carefully, the men harnessed the great tree to the back of the gigantic tractor, and very slowly they moved off.

After what seemed ages, they left the forest behind. They travelled slowly past the sawmill and went on into town.

As Creepy Crawler moved steadily through the streets, crowds of people stood cheering and waving.

"What's all this about?" Creepy Crawler shouted to the driver.

"Haven't you guessed?" the driver laughed. "The town is going to put up the biggest Christmas tree in the world right in the middle of the square, and you have brought it safely from the forest!"

Creepy Crawler felt very proud. In fact he blushed!

"There would be no Christmas tree without you!" shouted the crowd. They covered Creepy Crawler with trimmings, streamers and a long string of sparkling Christmas lights!